PASSWORD
LOG BOOK

THIS NOTEBOOK BELONGS TO

Name:..

Phone:...

Email:..

Address:..

A Password Log Book

Date

🌐 Website	
👤 Username	
✉ Email	
🔒 Password	
📝 Note	

🌐 Website	
👤 Username	
✉ Email	
🔒 Password	
📝 Note	

🌐 Website	
👤 Username	
✉ Email	
🔒 Password	
📝 Note	

🌐 Website	
👤 Username	
✉ Email	
🔒 Password	
📝 Note	

Password Log Book

🌐 Website	
👤 Username	
✉ Email	
🔒 Password	
📝 Note	

🌐 Website	
👤 Username	
✉ Email	
🔒 Password	
📝 Note	

🌐 Website	
👤 Username	
✉ Email	
🔒 Password	
📝 Note	

🌐 Website	
👤 Username	
✉ Email	
🔒 Password	
📝 Note	

A Password Log Book

Date

🌐 Website	
👤 Username	
✉ Email	
🔒 Password	
📝 Note	

🌐 Website	
👤 Username	
✉ Email	
🔒 Password	
📝 Note	

🌐 Website	
👤 Username	
✉ Email	
🔒 Password	
📝 Note	

🌐 Website	
👤 Username	
✉ Email	
🔒 Password	
📝 Note	

Password Log Book

Date

🌐 Website	
👤 Username	
✉ Email	
🔒 Password	
📝 Note	

🌐 Website	
👤 Username	
✉ Email	
🔒 Password	
📝 Note	

🌐 Website	
👤 Username	
✉ Email	
🔒 Password	
📝 Note	

🌐 Website	
👤 Username	
✉ Email	
🔒 Password	
📝 Note	

B Password Log Book

Date

🌐 Website	
👤 Username	
✉ Email	
🔒 Password	
📝 Note	

🌐 Website	
👤 Username	
✉ Email	
🔒 Password	
📝 Note	

🌐 Website	
👤 Username	
✉ Email	
🔒 Password	
📝 Note	

🌐 Website	
👤 Username	
✉ Email	
🔒 Password	
📝 Note	

Password Log Book

Date

🌐 Website	
👤 Username	
✉ Email	
🔒 Password	
📝 Note	

🌐 Website	
👤 Username	
✉ Email	
🔒 Password	
📝 Note	

🌐 Website	
👤 Username	
✉ Email	
🔒 Password	
📝 Note	

🌐 Website	
👤 Username	
✉ Email	
🔒 Password	
📝 Note	

Date ___________

🌐 Website	
👤 Username	
✉ Email	
🔒 Password	
📝 Note	

🌐 Website	
👤 Username	
✉ Email	
🔒 Password	
📝 Note	

🌐 Website	
👤 Username	
✉ Email	
🔒 Password	
📝 Note	

🌐 Website	
👤 Username	
✉ Email	
🔒 Password	
📝 Note	

Password Log Book

Date

Website	
Username	
Email	
Password	
Note	

Website	
Username	
Email	
Password	
Note	

Website	
Username	
Email	
Password	
Note	

Website	
Username	
Email	
Password	
Note	

🌐 **Website**	
👤 **Username**	
✉ **Email**	
🔒 **Password**	
📝 **Note**	

🌐 **Website**	
👤 **Username**	
✉ **Email**	
🔒 **Password**	
📝 **Note**	

🌐 **Website**	
👤 **Username**	
✉ **Email**	
🔒 **Password**	
📝 **Note**	

🌐 **Website**	
👤 **Username**	
✉ **Email**	
🔒 **Password**	
📝 **Note**	

Password Log Book

Date

🌐 Website	
👤 Username	
✉ Email	
🔒 Password	
📝 Note	

🌐 Website	
👤 Username	
✉ Email	
🔒 Password	
📝 Note	

🌐 Website	
👤 Username	
✉ Email	
🔒 Password	
📝 Note	

🌐 Website	
👤 Username	
✉ Email	
🔒 Password	
📝 Note	

C Password Log Book

Date

🌐 Website	
👤 Username	
✉ Email	
🔒 Password	
📝 Note	

🌐 Website	
👤 Username	
✉ Email	
🔒 Password	
📝 Note	

🌐 Website	
👤 Username	
✉ Email	
🔒 Password	
📝 Note	

🌐 Website	
👤 Username	
✉ Email	
🔒 Password	
📝 Note	

Password Log Book

Date

Website	
Username	
Email	
Password	
Note	

Website	
Username	
Email	
Password	
Note	

Website	
Username	
Email	
Password	
Note	

Website	
Username	
Email	
Password	
Note	

D Password Log Book

Date

🌐 Website	
👤 Username	
✉ Email	
🔒 Password	
📝 Note	

🌐 Website	
👤 Username	
✉ Email	
🔒 Password	
📝 Note	

🌐 Website	
👤 Username	
✉ Email	
🔒 Password	
📝 Note	

🌐 Website	
👤 Username	
✉ Email	
🔒 Password	
📝 Note	

Password Log Book

Date

🌐 Website	
👤 Username	
✉ Email	
🔒 Password	
📝 Note	

🌐 Website	
👤 Username	
✉ Email	
🔒 Password	
📝 Note	

🌐 Website	
👤 Username	
✉ Email	
🔒 Password	
📝 Note	

🌐 Website	
👤 Username	
✉ Email	
🔒 Password	
📝 Note	

D Password Log Book

Date

🌐 Website	
👤 Username	
✉ Email	
🔒 Password	
📝 Note	

🌐 Website	
👤 Username	
✉ Email	
🔒 Password	
📝 Note	

🌐 Website	
👤 Username	
✉ Email	
🔒 Password	
📝 Note	

🌐 Website	
👤 Username	
✉ Email	
🔒 Password	
📝 Note	

Password Log Book

Date

🌐 Website	
👤 Username	
✉ Email	
🔒 Password	
📓 Note	

🌐 Website	
👤 Username	
✉ Email	
🔒 Password	
📓 Note	

🌐 Website	
👤 Username	
✉ Email	
🔒 Password	
📓 Note	

🌐 Website	
👤 Username	
✉ Email	
🔒 Password	
📓 Note	

E Password Log Book

Date

🌐 Website	
👤 Username	
✉ Email	
🔒 Password	
📝 Note	

🌐 Website	
👤 Username	
✉ Email	
🔒 Password	
📝 Note	

🌐 Website	
👤 Username	
✉ Email	
🔒 Password	
📝 Note	

🌐 Website	
👤 Username	
✉ Email	
🔒 Password	
📝 Note	

Password Log Book

Date

🌐 Website	
👤 Username	
✉ Email	
🔒 Password	
📝 Note	

🌐 Website	
👤 Username	
✉ Email	
🔒 Password	
📝 Note	

🌐 Website	
👤 Username	
✉ Email	
🔒 Password	
📝 Note	

🌐 Website	
👤 Username	
✉ Email	
🔒 Password	
📝 Note	

E Password Log Book

Date

🌐 Website	
👤 Username	
✉ Email	
🔒 Password	
📝 Note	

🌐 Website	
👤 Username	
✉ Email	
🔒 Password	
📝 Note	

🌐 Website	
👤 Username	
✉ Email	
🔒 Password	
📝 Note	

🌐 Website	
👤 Username	
✉ Email	
🔒 Password	
📝 Note	

Password Log Book

Date

🌐 Website	
👤 Username	
✉ Email	
🔒 Password	
📝 Note	

🌐 Website	
👤 Username	
✉ Email	
🔒 Password	
📝 Note	

🌐 Website	
👤 Username	
✉ Email	
🔒 Password	
📝 Note	

🌐 Website	
👤 Username	
✉ Email	
🔒 Password	
📝 Note	

F Password Log Book   Date

🌐 Website	
👤 Username	
✉ Email	
🔒 Password	
📝 Note	

🌐 Website	
👤 Username	
✉ Email	
🔒 Password	
📝 Note	

🌐 Website	
👤 Username	
✉ Email	
🔒 Password	
📝 Note	

🌐 Website	
👤 Username	
✉ Email	
🔒 Password	
📝 Note	

Password Log Book

Date

Website	
Username	
Email	
Password	
Note	

Website	
Username	
Email	
Password	
Note	

Website	
Username	
Email	
Password	
Note	

Website	
Username	
Email	
Password	
Note	

F Password Log Book

Date

🌐 Website	
👤 Username	
✉ Email	
🔒 Password	
📝 Note	

🌐 Website	
👤 Username	
✉ Email	
🔒 Password	
📝 Note	

🌐 Website	
👤 Username	
✉ Email	
🔒 Password	
📝 Note	

🌐 Website	
👤 Username	
✉ Email	
🔒 Password	
📝 Note	

Password Log Book

Date

🌐 Website	
👤 Username	
✉ Email	
🔒 Password	
📝 Note	

🌐 Website	
👤 Username	
✉ Email	
🔒 Password	
📝 Note	

🌐 Website	
👤 Username	
✉ Email	
🔒 Password	
📝 Note	

🌐 Website	
👤 Username	
✉ Email	
🔒 Password	
📝 Note	

G Password Log Book

Date

🌐 Website	
👤 Username	
✉ Email	
🔒 Password	
📝 Note	

🌐 Website	
👤 Username	
✉ Email	
🔒 Password	
📝 Note	

🌐 Website	
👤 Username	
✉ Email	
🔒 Password	
📝 Note	

🌐 Website	
👤 Username	
✉ Email	
🔒 Password	
📝 Note	

Password Log Book

Date

🌐 Website	
👤 Username	
✉ Email	
🔒 Password	
📝 Note	

🌐 Website	
👤 Username	
✉ Email	
🔒 Password	
📝 Note	

🌐 Website	
👤 Username	
✉ Email	
🔒 Password	
📝 Note	

🌐 Website	
👤 Username	
✉ Email	
🔒 Password	
📝 Note	

Password Log Book

Date

🌐 Website	
👤 Username	
✉ Email	
🔒 Password	
📝 Note	

🌐 Website	
👤 Username	
✉ Email	
🔒 Password	
📝 Note	

🌐 Website	
👤 Username	
✉ Email	
🔒 Password	
📝 Note	

🌐 Website	
👤 Username	
✉ Email	
🔒 Password	
📝 Note	

Password Log Book

Date

🌐 Website	
👤 Username	
✉ Email	
🔒 Password	
📝 Note	

🌐 Website	
👤 Username	
✉ Email	
🔒 Password	
📝 Note	

🌐 Website	
👤 Username	
✉ Email	
🔒 Password	
📝 Note	

🌐 Website	
👤 Username	
✉ Email	
🔒 Password	
📝 Note	

▚ Password Log Book

🌐 Website	
👤 Username	
✉ Email	
🔒 Password	
📝 Note	

🌐 Website	
👤 Username	
✉ Email	
🔒 Password	
📝 Note	

🌐 Website	
👤 Username	
✉ Email	
🔒 Password	
📝 Note	

🌐 Website	
👤 Username	
✉ Email	
🔒 Password	
📝 Note	

Password Log Book

Date

🌐 Website	
👤 Username	
✉ Email	
🔒 Password	
📝 Note	

🌐 Website	
👤 Username	
✉ Email	
🔒 Password	
📝 Note	

🌐 Website	
👤 Username	
✉ Email	
🔒 Password	
📝 Note	

🌐 Website	
👤 Username	
✉ Email	
🔒 Password	
📝 Note	

H Password Log Book

Date

🌐 Website	
👤 Username	
✉ Email	
🔒 Password	
📝 Note	

🌐 Website	
👤 Username	
✉ Email	
🔒 Password	
📝 Note	

🌐 Website	
👤 Username	
✉ Email	
🔒 Password	
📝 Note	

🌐 Website	
👤 Username	
✉ Email	
🔒 Password	
📝 Note	

Password Log Book

Date

🌐 Website	
👤 Username	
✉ Email	
🔒 Password	
📝 Note	

🌐 Website	
👤 Username	
✉ Email	
🔒 Password	
📝 Note	

🌐 Website	
👤 Username	
✉ Email	
🔒 Password	
📝 Note	

🌐 Website	
👤 Username	
✉ Email	
🔒 Password	
📝 Note	

🌐 Website	
👤 Username	
✉ Email	
🔒 Password	
📝 Note	

🌐 Website	
👤 Username	
✉ Email	
🔒 Password	
📝 Note	

🌐 Website	
👤 Username	
✉ Email	
🔒 Password	
📝 Note	

🌐 Website	
👤 Username	
✉ Email	
🔒 Password	
📝 Note	

Password Log Book

Date

🌐 Website	
👤 Username	
✉ Email	
🔒 Password	
📝 Note	

🌐 Website	
👤 Username	
✉ Email	
🔒 Password	
📝 Note	

🌐 Website	
👤 Username	
✉ Email	
🔒 Password	
📝 Note	

🌐 Website	
👤 Username	
✉ Email	
🔒 Password	
📝 Note	

Password Log Book

Date

🌐 Website	
👤 Username	
✉ Email	
🔒 Password	
📝 Note	

🌐 Website	
👤 Username	
✉ Email	
🔒 Password	
📝 Note	

🌐 Website	
👤 Username	
✉ Email	
🔒 Password	
📝 Note	

🌐 Website	
👤 Username	
✉ Email	
🔒 Password	
📝 Note	

Password Log Book

Date

🌐 Website	
👤 Username	
✉ Email	
🔒 Password	
📝 Note	

🌐 Website	
👤 Username	
✉ Email	
🔒 Password	
📝 Note	

🌐 Website	
👤 Username	
✉ Email	
🔒 Password	
📝 Note	

🌐 Website	
👤 Username	
✉ Email	
🔒 Password	
📝 Note	

Password Log Book

Date

🌐 Website	
👤 Username	
✉ Email	
🔒 Password	
📝 Note	

🌐 Website	
👤 Username	
✉ Email	
🔒 Password	
📝 Note	

🌐 Website	
👤 Username	
✉ Email	
🔒 Password	
📝 Note	

🌐 Website	
👤 Username	
✉ Email	
🔒 Password	
📝 Note	

J Password Log Book

Date

🌐 Website	
👤 Username	
✉ Email	
🔒 Password	
📝 Note	

🌐 Website	
👤 Username	
✉ Email	
🔒 Password	
📝 Note	

🌐 Website	
👤 Username	
✉ Email	
🔒 Password	
📝 Note	

🌐 Website	
👤 Username	
✉ Email	
🔒 Password	
📝 Note	

🌐 Website	
👤 Username	
✉ Email	
🔒 Password	
📝 Note	

🌐 Website	
👤 Username	
✉ Email	
🔒 Password	
📝 Note	

🌐 Website	
👤 Username	
✉ Email	
🔒 Password	
📝 Note	

🌐 Website	
👤 Username	
✉ Email	
🔒 Password	
📝 Note	

Password Log Book

Date

Website	
Username	
Email	
Password	
Note	

Website	
Username	
Email	
Password	
Note	

Website	
Username	
Email	
Password	
Note	

Website	
Username	
Email	
Password	
Note	

K Password Log Book

Date

🌐 Website	
👤 Username	
✉ Email	
🔒 Password	
📝 Note	

🌐 Website	
👤 Username	
✉ Email	
🔒 Password	
📝 Note	

🌐 Website	
👤 Username	
✉ Email	
🔒 Password	
📝 Note	

🌐 Website	
👤 Username	
✉ Email	
🔒 Password	
📝 Note	

Website	
Username	
Email	
Password	
Note	

Website	
Username	
Email	
Password	
Note	

Website	
Username	
Email	
Password	
Note	

Website	
Username	
Email	
Password	
Note	

K Password Log Book

Date

🌐 Website	
👤 Username	
✉ Email	
🔒 Password	
📝 Note	

🌐 Website	
👤 Username	
✉ Email	
🔒 Password	
📝 Note	

🌐 Website	
👤 Username	
✉ Email	
🔒 Password	
📝 Note	

🌐 Website	
👤 Username	
✉ Email	
🔒 Password	
📝 Note	

K Password Log Book   Date

	Website
👤	Username
✉	Email
🔒	Password
📝	Note

	Website
👤	Username
✉	Email
🔒	Password
📝	Note

	Website
👤	Username
✉	Email
🔒	Password
📝	Note

	Website
👤	Username
✉	Email
🔒	Password
📝	Note

Password Log Book

Date

🌐 Website	
👤 Username	
✉ Email	
🔒 Password	
📝 Note	

🌐 Website	
👤 Username	
✉ Email	
🔒 Password	
📝 Note	

🌐 Website	
👤 Username	
✉ Email	
🔒 Password	
📝 Note	

🌐 Website	
👤 Username	
✉ Email	
🔒 Password	
📝 Note	

Password Log Book

Date

🌐 Website	
👤 Username	
✉ Email	
🔒 Password	
📝 Note	

🌐 Website	
👤 Username	
✉ Email	
🔒 Password	
📝 Note	

🌐 Website	
👤 Username	
✉ Email	
🔒 Password	
📝 Note	

🌐 Website	
👤 Username	
✉ Email	
🔒 Password	
📝 Note	

Date

🌐 Website	
👤 Username	
✉ Email	
🔒 Password	
📝 Note	

🌐 Website	
👤 Username	
✉ Email	
🔒 Password	
📝 Note	

🌐 Website	
👤 Username	
✉ Email	
🔒 Password	
📝 Note	

🌐 Website	
👤 Username	
✉ Email	
🔒 Password	
📝 Note	

Password Log Book

Date

🌐 Website	
👤 Username	
✉ Email	
🔒 Password	
📝 Note	

🌐 Website	
👤 Username	
✉ Email	
🔒 Password	
📝 Note	

🌐 Website	
👤 Username	
✉ Email	
🔒 Password	
📝 Note	

🌐 Website	
👤 Username	
✉ Email	
🔒 Password	
📝 Note	

🌐 Website	
👤 Username	
✉ Email	
🔒 Password	
📝 Note	

🌐 Website	
👤 Username	
✉ Email	
🔒 Password	
📝 Note	

🌐 Website	
👤 Username	
✉ Email	
🔒 Password	
📝 Note	

🌐 Website	
👤 Username	
✉ Email	
🔒 Password	
📝 Note	

Password Log Book

Date

Website	
Username	
Email	
Password	
Note	

Website	
Username	
Email	
Password	
Note	

Website	
Username	
Email	
Password	
Note	

Website	
Username	
Email	
Password	
Note	

M Password Log Book

Date

🌐 Website	
👤 Username	
✉ Email	
🔒 Password	
📝 Note	

🌐 Website	
👤 Username	
✉ Email	
🔒 Password	
📝 Note	

🌐 Website	
👤 Username	
✉ Email	
🔒 Password	
📝 Note	

🌐 Website	
👤 Username	
✉ Email	
🔒 Password	
📝 Note	

Password Log Book

Date

🌐 Website	
👤 Username	
✉ Email	
🔒 Password	
📝 Note	

🌐 Website	
👤 Username	
✉ Email	
🔒 Password	
📝 Note	

🌐 Website	
👤 Username	
✉ Email	
🔒 Password	
📝 Note	

🌐 Website	
👤 Username	
✉ Email	
🔒 Password	
📝 Note	

N Password Log Book

Date

🌐 Website	
👤 Username	
✉ Email	
🔒 Password	
📝 Note	

🌐 Website	
👤 Username	
✉ Email	
🔒 Password	
📝 Note	

🌐 Website	
👤 Username	
✉ Email	
🔒 Password	
📝 Note	

🌐 Website	
👤 Username	
✉ Email	
🔒 Password	
📝 Note	

Password Log Book

🌐 Website	
👤 Username	
✉ Email	
🔒 Password	
📝 Note	

🌐 Website	
👤 Username	
✉ Email	
🔒 Password	
📝 Note	

🌐 Website	
👤 Username	
✉ Email	
🔒 Password	
📝 Note	

🌐 Website	
👤 Username	
✉ Email	
🔒 Password	
📝 Note	

🌐 Website	
👤 Username	
✉ Email	
🔒 Password	
📝 Note	

🌐 Website	
👤 Username	
✉ Email	
🔒 Password	
📝 Note	

🌐 Website	
👤 Username	
✉ Email	
🔒 Password	
📝 Note	

🌐 Website	
👤 Username	
✉ Email	
🔒 Password	
📝 Note	

N Password Log Book

Date

🌐 Website	
👤 Username	
✉ Email	
🔒 Password	
📝 Note	

🌐 Website	
👤 Username	
✉ Email	
🔒 Password	
📝 Note	

🌐 Website	
👤 Username	
✉ Email	
🔒 Password	
📝 Note	

🌐 Website	
👤 Username	
✉ Email	
🔒 Password	
📝 Note	

Date

🌐 Website	
👤 Username	
✉ Email	
🔒 Password	
📝 Note	

🌐 Website	
👤 Username	
✉ Email	
🔒 Password	
📝 Note	

🌐 Website	
👤 Username	
✉ Email	
🔒 Password	
📝 Note	

🌐 Website	
👤 Username	
✉ Email	
🔒 Password	
📝 Note	

Password Log Book

Date

🌐 Website	
👤 Username	
✉ Email	
🔒 Password	
📝 Note	

🌐 Website	
👤 Username	
✉ Email	
🔒 Password	
📝 Note	

🌐 Website	
👤 Username	
✉ Email	
🔒 Password	
📝 Note	

🌐 Website	
👤 Username	
✉ Email	
🔒 Password	
📝 Note	

Password Log Book

Date

Website	
Username	
Email	
Password	
Note	

Website	
Username	
Email	
Password	
Note	

Website	
Username	
Email	
Password	
Note	

Website	
Username	
Email	
Password	
Note	

Password Log Book

Date

🌐 Website	
👤 Username	
✉ Email	
🔒 Password	
📝 Note	

🌐 Website	
👤 Username	
✉ Email	
🔒 Password	
📝 Note	

🌐 Website	
👤 Username	
✉ Email	
🔒 Password	
📝 Note	

🌐 Website	
👤 Username	
✉ Email	
🔒 Password	
📝 Note	

	Website
	Username
	Email
	Password
	Note

	Website
	Username
	Email
	Password
	Note

	Website
	Username
	Email
	Password
	Note

	Website
	Username
	Email
	Password
	Note

P Password Log Book

Date

🌐 Website	
👤 Username	
✉ Email	
🔒 Password	
📝 Note	

🌐 Website	
👤 Username	
✉ Email	
🔒 Password	
📝 Note	

🌐 Website	
👤 Username	
✉ Email	
🔒 Password	
📝 Note	

🌐 Website	
👤 Username	
✉ Email	
🔒 Password	
📝 Note	

P # Password Log Book   Date

🌐 Website	
👤 Username	
✉ Email	
🔒 Password	
📝 Note	

🌐 Website	
👤 Username	
✉ Email	
🔒 Password	
📝 Note	

🌐 Website	
👤 Username	
✉ Email	
🔒 Password	
📝 Note	

🌐 Website	
👤 Username	
✉ Email	
🔒 Password	
📝 Note	

P Password Log Book

Date

🌐 Website	
👤 Username	
✉ Email	
🔒 Password	
📝 Note	

🌐 Website	
👤 Username	
✉ Email	
🔒 Password	
📝 Note	

🌐 Website	
👤 Username	
✉ Email	
🔒 Password	
📝 Note	

🌐 Website	
👤 Username	
✉ Email	
🔒 Password	
📝 Note	

🌐 Website	
👤 Username	
✉ Email	
🔒 Password	
📝 Note	

🌐 Website	
👤 Username	
✉ Email	
🔒 Password	
📝 Note	

🌐 Website	
👤 Username	
✉ Email	
🔒 Password	
📝 Note	

🌐 Website	
👤 Username	
✉ Email	
🔒 Password	
📝 Note	

Password Log Book

Date

🌐 **Website**	
👤 **Username**	
✉ **Email**	
🔒 **Password**	
📝 **Note**	

🌐 **Website**	
👤 **Username**	
✉ **Email**	
🔒 **Password**	
📝 **Note**	

🌐 **Website**	
👤 **Username**	
✉ **Email**	
🔒 **Password**	
📝 **Note**	

🌐 **Website**	
👤 **Username**	
✉ **Email**	
🔒 **Password**	
📝 **Note**	

Q Password Log Book

Date

🌐 Website	
👤 Username	
✉ Email	
🔒 Password	
📝 Note	

🌐 Website	
👤 Username	
✉ Email	
🔒 Password	
📝 Note	

🌐 Website	
👤 Username	
✉ Email	
🔒 Password	
📝 Note	

🌐 Website	
👤 Username	
✉ Email	
🔒 Password	
📝 Note	

⊕ Website	
👤 Username	
✉ Email	
🔒 Password	
📝 Note	

⊕ Website	
👤 Username	
✉ Email	
🔒 Password	
📝 Note	

⊕ Website	
👤 Username	
✉ Email	
🔒 Password	
📝 Note	

⊕ Website	
👤 Username	
✉ Email	
🔒 Password	
📝 Note	

R Password Log Book

Date

🌐 Website	
👤 Username	
✉ Email	
🔒 Password	
📝 Note	

🌐 Website	
👤 Username	
✉ Email	
🔒 Password	
📝 Note	

🌐 Website	
👤 Username	
✉ Email	
🔒 Password	
📝 Note	

🌐 Website	
👤 Username	
✉ Email	
🔒 Password	
📝 Note	

Password Log Book

Date

🌐 Website	
👤 Username	
✉ Email	
🔒 Password	
📝 Note	

🌐 Website	
👤 Username	
✉ Email	
🔒 Password	
📝 Note	

🌐 Website	
👤 Username	
✉ Email	
🔒 Password	
📝 Note	

🌐 Website	
👤 Username	
✉ Email	
🔒 Password	
📝 Note	

R Password Log Book

Date

🌐 Website	
👤 Username	
✉ Email	
🔒 Password	
📝 Note	

🌐 Website	
👤 Username	
✉ Email	
🔒 Password	
📝 Note	

🌐 Website	
👤 Username	
✉ Email	
🔒 Password	
📝 Note	

🌐 Website	
👤 Username	
✉ Email	
🔒 Password	
📝 Note	

Password Log Book

Date

🌐 Website	
👤 Username	
✉ Email	
🔒 Password	
📝 Note	

🌐 Website	
👤 Username	
✉ Email	
🔒 Password	
📝 Note	

🌐 Website	
👤 Username	
✉ Email	
🔒 Password	
📝 Note	

🌐 Website	
👤 Username	
✉ Email	
🔒 Password	
📝 Note	

🌐 Website	
👤 Username	
✉ Email	
🔒 Password	
📝 Note	

🌐 Website	
👤 Username	
✉ Email	
🔒 Password	
📝 Note	

🌐 Website	
👤 Username	
✉ Email	
🔒 Password	
📝 Note	

🌐 Website	
👤 Username	
✉ Email	
🔒 Password	
📝 Note	

Password Log Book

Date

🌐 Website	
👤 Username	
✉ Email	
🔒 Password	
📝 Note	

🌐 Website	
👤 Username	
✉ Email	
🔒 Password	
📝 Note	

🌐 Website	
👤 Username	
✉ Email	
🔒 Password	
📝 Note	

🌐 Website	
👤 Username	
✉ Email	
🔒 Password	
📝 Note	

🌐 Website	
👤 Username	
✉ Email	
🔒 Password	
📝 Note	

🌐 Website	
👤 Username	
✉ Email	
🔒 Password	
📝 Note	

🌐 Website	
👤 Username	
✉ Email	
🔒 Password	
📝 Note	

🌐 Website	
👤 Username	
✉ Email	
🔒 Password	
📝 Note	

🌐 Website	
👤 Username	
✉ Email	
🔒 Password	
📝 Note	

🌐 Website	
👤 Username	
✉ Email	
🔒 Password	
📝 Note	

🌐 Website	
👤 Username	
✉ Email	
🔒 Password	
📝 Note	

🌐 Website	
👤 Username	
✉ Email	
🔒 Password	
📝 Note	

Password Log Book

Date

🌐 Website	
👤 Username	
✉ Email	
🔒 Password	
📝 Note	

🌐 Website	
👤 Username	
✉ Email	
🔒 Password	
📝 Note	

🌐 Website	
👤 Username	
✉ Email	
🔒 Password	
📝 Note	

🌐 Website	
👤 Username	
✉ Email	
🔒 Password	
📝 Note	

Password Log Book

Date

🌐 Website	
👤 Username	
✉ Email	
🔒 Password	
📝 Note	

🌐 Website	
👤 Username	
✉ Email	
🔒 Password	
📝 Note	

🌐 Website	
👤 Username	
✉ Email	
🔒 Password	
📝 Note	

🌐 Website	
👤 Username	
✉ Email	
🔒 Password	
📝 Note	

🄣 Password Log Book

Date

🌐 Website	
👤 Username	
✉ Email	
🔒 Password	
📝 Note	

🌐 Website	
👤 Username	
✉ Email	
🔒 Password	
📝 Note	

🌐 Website	
👤 Username	
✉ Email	
🔒 Password	
📝 Note	

🌐 Website	
👤 Username	
✉ Email	
🔒 Password	
📝 Note	

Password Log Book

Date

🌐 Website	
👤 Username	
✉ Email	
🔒 Password	
📝 Note	

🌐 Website	
👤 Username	
✉ Email	
🔒 Password	
📝 Note	

🌐 Website	
👤 Username	
✉ Email	
🔒 Password	
📝 Note	

🌐 Website	
👤 Username	
✉ Email	
🔒 Password	
📝 Note	

Password Log Book

Date

🌐 Website	
👤 Username	
✉ Email	
🔒 Password	
📝 Note	

🌐 Website	
👤 Username	
✉ Email	
🔒 Password	
📝 Note	

🌐 Website	
👤 Username	
✉ Email	
🔒 Password	
📝 Note	

🌐 Website	
👤 Username	
✉ Email	
🔒 Password	
📝 Note	

U Password Log Book — Date ______

Website	
Username	
Email	
Password	
Note	

Website	
Username	
Email	
Password	
Note	

Website	
Username	
Email	
Password	
Note	

Website	
Username	
Email	
Password	
Note	

🌐 Website	
👤 Username	
✉ Email	
🔒 Password	
📝 Note	

🌐 Website	
👤 Username	
✉ Email	
🔒 Password	
📝 Note	

🌐 Website	
👤 Username	
✉ Email	
🔒 Password	
📝 Note	

🌐 Website	
👤 Username	
✉ Email	
🔒 Password	
📝 Note	

Password Log Book

<table>
<tr><td>U</td><td colspan="2">Password Log Book</td><td>Date</td></tr>
</table>

🌐 Website	
👤 Username	
✉ Email	
🔒 Password	
📝 Note	

🌐 Website	
👤 Username	
✉ Email	
🔒 Password	
📝 Note	

🌐 Website	
👤 Username	
✉ Email	
🔒 Password	
📝 Note	

🌐 Website	
👤 Username	
✉ Email	
🔒 Password	
📝 Note	

V Password Log Book

Date

🌐 Website	
👤 Username	
✉ Email	
🔒 Password	
📝 Note	

🌐 Website	
👤 Username	
✉ Email	
🔒 Password	
📝 Note	

🌐 Website	
👤 Username	
✉ Email	
🔒 Password	
📝 Note	

🌐 Website	
👤 Username	
✉ Email	
🔒 Password	
📝 Note	

V Password Log Book

Date

🌐 Website	
👤 Username	
✉ Email	
🔒 Password	
📝 Note	

🌐 Website	
👤 Username	
✉ Email	
🔒 Password	
📝 Note	

🌐 Website	
👤 Username	
✉ Email	
🔒 Password	
📝 Note	

🌐 Website	
👤 Username	
✉ Email	
🔒 Password	
📝 Note	

🌐 Website	
👤 Username	
✉ Email	
🔒 Password	
📝 Note	

🌐 Website	
👤 Username	
✉ Email	
🔒 Password	
📝 Note	

🌐 Website	
👤 Username	
✉ Email	
🔒 Password	
📝 Note	

🌐 Website	
👤 Username	
✉ Email	
🔒 Password	
📝 Note	

V Password Log Book

Date

🌐 Website	
👤 Username	
✉ Email	
🔒 Password	
📝 Note	

🌐 Website	
👤 Username	
✉ Email	
🔒 Password	
📝 Note	

🌐 Website	
👤 Username	
✉ Email	
🔒 Password	
📝 Note	

🌐 Website	
👤 Username	
✉ Email	
🔒 Password	
📝 Note	

W Password Log Book

Date

🌐 Website	
👤 Username	
✉ Email	
🔒 Password	
📝 Note	

🌐 Website	
👤 Username	
✉ Email	
🔒 Password	
📝 Note	

🌐 Website	
👤 Username	
✉ Email	
🔒 Password	
📝 Note	

🌐 Website	
👤 Username	
✉ Email	
🔒 Password	
📝 Note	

🌐 Website	
👤 Username	
✉ Email	
🔒 Password	
📝 Note	

🌐 Website	
👤 Username	
✉ Email	
🔒 Password	
📝 Note	

🌐 Website	
👤 Username	
✉ Email	
🔒 Password	
📝 Note	

🌐 Website	
👤 Username	
✉ Email	
🔒 Password	
📝 Note	

W Password Log Book

Date

🌐 Website	
👤 Username	
✉ Email	
🔒 Password	
📝 Note	

🌐 Website	
👤 Username	
✉ Email	
🔒 Password	
📝 Note	

🌐 Website	
👤 Username	
✉ Email	
🔒 Password	
📝 Note	

🌐 Website	
👤 Username	
✉ Email	
🔒 Password	
📝 Note	

W Password Log Book

Date

🌐 Website	
👤 Username	
✉ Email	
🔒 Password	
📝 Note	

🌐 Website	
👤 Username	
✉ Email	
🔒 Password	
📝 Note	

🌐 Website	
👤 Username	
✉ Email	
🔒 Password	
📝 Note	

🌐 Website	
👤 Username	
✉ Email	
🔒 Password	
📝 Note	

🌐 Website	
👤 Username	
✉ Email	
🔒 Password	
📝 Note	

🌐 Website	
👤 Username	
✉ Email	
🔒 Password	
📝 Note	

🌐 Website	
👤 Username	
✉ Email	
🔒 Password	
📝 Note	

🌐 Website	
👤 Username	
✉ Email	
🔒 Password	
📝 Note	

🌐 Website	
👤 Username	
✉ Email	
🔒 Password	
📝 Note	

🌐 Website	
👤 Username	
✉ Email	
🔒 Password	
📝 Note	

🌐 Website	
👤 Username	
✉ Email	
🔒 Password	
📝 Note	

🌐 Website	
👤 Username	
✉ Email	
🔒 Password	
📝 Note	

X Password Log Book

Date

🌐 Website	
👤 Username	
✉ Email	
🔒 Password	
📝 Note	

🌐 Website	
👤 Username	
✉ Email	
🔒 Password	
📝 Note	

🌐 Website	
👤 Username	
✉ Email	
🔒 Password	
📝 Note	

🌐 Website	
👤 Username	
✉ Email	
🔒 Password	
📝 Note	

X Password Log Book

Date

🌐 Website	
👤 Username	
✉ Email	
🔒 Password	
📝 Note	

🌐 Website	
👤 Username	
✉ Email	
🔒 Password	
📝 Note	

🌐 Website	
👤 Username	
✉ Email	
🔒 Password	
📝 Note	

🌐 Website	
👤 Username	
✉ Email	
🔒 Password	
📝 Note	

🌐 Website	
👤 Username	
✉ Email	
🔒 Password	
📝 Note	

🌐 Website	
👤 Username	
✉ Email	
🔒 Password	
📝 Note	

🌐 Website	
👤 Username	
✉ Email	
🔒 Password	
📝 Note	

🌐 Website	
👤 Username	
✉ Email	
🔒 Password	
📝 Note	

Password Log Book

Date

🌐 Website	
👤 Username	
✉ Email	
🔒 Password	
📝 Note	

🌐 Website	
👤 Username	
✉ Email	
🔒 Password	
📝 Note	

🌐 Website	
👤 Username	
✉ Email	
🔒 Password	
📝 Note	

🌐 Website	
👤 Username	
✉ Email	
🔒 Password	
📝 Note	

Password Log Book

Date

🌐 Website	
👤 Username	
✉ Email	
🔒 Password	
📝 Note	

🌐 Website	
👤 Username	
✉ Email	
🔒 Password	
📝 Note	

🌐 Website	
👤 Username	
✉ Email	
🔒 Password	
📝 Note	

🌐 Website	
👤 Username	
✉ Email	
🔒 Password	
📝 Note	

🌐 Website	
👤 Username	
✉ Email	
🔒 Password	
📝 Note	

🌐 Website	
👤 Username	
✉ Email	
🔒 Password	
📝 Note	

🌐 Website	
👤 Username	
✉ Email	
🔒 Password	
📝 Note	

🌐 Website	
👤 Username	
✉ Email	
🔒 Password	
📝 Note	

🌐 Website	
👤 Username	
✉ Email	
🔒 Password	
📝 Note	

🌐 Website	
👤 Username	
✉ Email	
🔒 Password	
📝 Note	

🌐 Website	
👤 Username	
✉ Email	
🔒 Password	
📝 Note	

🌐 Website	
👤 Username	
✉ Email	
🔒 Password	
📝 Note	

Z Password Log Book

Date

🌐 Website	
👤 Username	
✉ Email	
🔒 Password	
📝 Note	

🌐 Website	
👤 Username	
✉ Email	
🔒 Password	
📝 Note	

🌐 Website	
👤 Username	
✉ Email	
🔒 Password	
📝 Note	

🌐 Website	
👤 Username	
✉ Email	
🔒 Password	
📝 Note	

🌐 Website	
👤 Username	
✉ Email	
🔒 Password	
📝 Note	

🌐 Website	
👤 Username	
✉ Email	
🔒 Password	
📝 Note	

🌐 Website	
👤 Username	
✉ Email	
🔒 Password	
📝 Note	

🌐 Website	
👤 Username	
✉ Email	
🔒 Password	
📝 Note	